Elder Oliveira

# Installing Landscapes

## Design and Performance of Sound Installations for Specific Places



ScienciaScripts

**Imprint**



Cover image: www.ingimage.com

This book is a translation from the original published under ISBN 978-3-330-19940-8.

Publisher:
Sciencia Scripts
is a trademark of
Dodo Books Indian Ocean Ltd. and OmniScriptum S.R.L publishing group

120 High Road, East Finchley, London, N2 9ED, United Kingdom
Str. Armeneasca 28/1, office 1, Chisinau MD-2012, Republic of Moldova, Europe
Printed at: see last page
**ISBN: 978-620-8-25833-7**

Elder Oliveira

# Installing Landscapes

# SUMMARY


| | |
|---|---|
| Chapter 1 | 2 |
| Chapter 2 | 3 |
| Chapter 3 | 6 |
| Chapter 4 | 11 |
| Chapter 5 | 13 |
| Chapter 6 | 15 |
| Chapter 7 | 22 |
| Chapter 8 | 39 |
| Chapter 9 | 42 |

# 1 SOUND INSTALLATION

O study that relates the theoretical referential about sound installations and the soundscape points out, firstly, that the relationship between sound and space is fundamental in sound art and for the composition of sound installations created for a specific place. Another pertinent issue is the relationship between sound installation and the visual arts, and the relationship that is created between sound, image and time. In this way, this hybrid art form relates to various disciplines and, by relating to sculpture, architecture, expanded cinema and ecology, it proposes an interactive composition and audience, integrated with the acoustic and visual realities of the broadcasting spaces. In this way, this document presents the relationships between the concepts of sound installation and space, semiotics and hermeneutics, spectromorphology and psychoacoustics. It also presents a brief analysis of my sound installations *'Spiritual Convergence'* (2014) and *'Saving Shapes'* (2017), relating them to the body of work on the soundscape (Schaffer (1977), Westerkamp (1988), Westerkamp (1996) and Truax (1996); a first look at the relationship between the process of recording the soundscape in motion during the artistic-ecological act of *soundwalking* and sound art, with a view to new possibilities for creation and dissemination.

## 2 Sound installation, Sound, Space and Time

Initially, approaching soundscape content from the perspective of sound art means relating the sounds that make up a given space, considering the components of the landscape in their entirety. As far as sound installations are concerned, for Bandt (2006) sound installations are rarely static, presenting various exhibition possibilities and a high degree of involvement on the part of those present. The malleability of the exhibition encourages a specific study of the formats for disseminating a sound installation. Depending on the artist's creativity, movement can be explored in countless ways and provide different types of involvement between the work and the recipient. Thus, it becomes a fundamental part of the research to point out the composer's criteria for choosing the tools that are necessary to meet their artistic needs. In this case, following Bandt's logic, it is also necessary to reflect on what a static sound installation is and how it can involve those present at an exhibition.

Firstly, Bandt (2006) presents a first definition of sound installation by Max Neuhaus, who defines that *"Sound installation can be defined as a place, which has been spatially articulated with sound elements for the purpose of listening over a long period of time"* (BANDT, 2006:353, author's translation)[1] . On the other hand, he himself argues that "Sound installation is a hybrid art form, non-linear, flexible and temporal, with many inputs and outputs. It's no surprise that sound installations exist in many forms" (BANDT, 2006:354)[2] . Essentially, a sound installation can survive over a long period of time, being active for months or even years. However, a sound installation does not need to exist for long periods. This mode of intervention can be much more ephemeral, depending on the creativity and artistic intentions of the composer, knowing the conceptual construction that choices about time can have on an artistic work.

Therefore, a first aesthetic consideration offered by Bandt (2006) is that

> "The *path o qua! o artist Integrates the sculpture of sound, its dispersion in space and the visual integration como a whole for o architected space, tai como in a cultural enclosure, build or break with a work"* (BANDT, 2006:359) .[3]

---

1 "Sound installation can be defined as a place, which has been articulated spatially with sounding elements for the purpose of listening over a long time span" (BANDT, 2006:353).
2 "Sound installation is a non-linear, flexible and temporal hybrid artform, with many entrances and exits. It is not surprising that sound installations exist in many forms" (BANDT, 2006:354).
3 "The way the artist integrates the sculpting of sound, its dispersion in the space and the overall visual integration to the architectural space and cultural precinct makes or breaks a work" (BANDT, 2006:359).

In a sound installation, the artistic content is projected as a whole, taking into account the visual characteristics of the medium; the objects present, as well as the acoustic characteristics of the exhibition venue, considering the aesthetic charge that is composed from the composer's decision-making.

In the same way, knowing that each space provides a set of specific conditions that contribute to or limit artistic making, Melinda Barlow (1995) points out that Mary Lucier explored the space, even knowing the limitations that a multimedia presentation contained in the 70s. She also points out that she took advantage of the relationship between human beings and the landscape to build her installations. Thus, admitting the force of the constraints of the space that act on the work of art and making it possible to control these parameters, or the impossibility of acting on these parameters, to which a work of art is subjected.

On the other hand, in relation specifically to electroacoustic music, Smalley (2000) points out the importance of sound diffusion for the reception of the characteristics of the space by the receiver, *"Sound diffusion is the projection and spreading of sound in an acoustic space to a group of listeners - as opposed to listening in a private space (living room, office or study)"* (AUSTIN, 2000:10)[4] . Another definition pointed out by him is that sound diffusion can be *"(...) the 'sonorization' of an acoustic space and the optimization of the format and structure of sound to create a rewarding listening experience"* (AUSTIN, 2000:10)[5] . In this way, aware of the growing need to optimize sound diffusion in order to take advantage of the acoustic characteristics of concert halls, galleries and open-air exhibitions, composers composed works for specific venues, taking advantage of certain acoustic characteristics of the place. Contrary to this type of procedure in electroacoustic music, Smalley (2000) suggests that the

> *"(...) electroacoustic music is not necessarily composed from listening to a specific space in mind - not necessarily and not usually. Music must be adapted to accept the particularity of performance spaces"* (AUSTIN, 2000:11) .[6]

Thus, knowing that each space has a series of variants that contribute to altering the

4 "Sound diffusion is the projection and the spreading of sound in an acoustic space for a group of Listeners - as opposed to listening in a personal space (living room, office, orstudio)" (AUSTIN, 2000:10).
5 (...) the 'sonorizing' of the acoustic space and the enhancing of sound-shapes and structure in order to create a rewarding Listening experience" (AUSTIN, 2000:10).
6 "(...) electroacoustic music is not necessarily composed with the specific listening space in mind - not necessarily, and not usually. The music has to be adapted to suit the particular performance space" (AUSTIN, 2000:11).

perception of sound, Smalley (2000) presents five variants that stand out in the transformation of sound diffusion: 1. proximity or distance; 2. superficiality or depth; 3. image definition or localization (composed of a textural definition or a trajectorial drama); 4. orientation (composed of a multidirectional or frontal sensation); and 5. spectral quality. On the other hand, emphasizing the appropriation of the external space for musical composition and for the exhibition of sound installations, Smalley defines the external space as a perspective that can have different dimensions: 1. open or delimited spaces; 2. closed or intimate spaces; and 3. wide or shallow spaces. Finally, Smalley points out the six topics that help define a global spatial style: 1. simple spatial configuration; 2. multiple spatial configuration; 3. spatial simultaneity; 4. implied spatial simultaneity; 5. spatial passage; and, 6. spatial balance. These topics serve as tools for understanding and experiencing sound phenomena. They also help communication between composer and listener, narrowing the gap that a new musical language sustains.

## 3 Sound installation, Semiotics and Hermeneutics

The influence of semiotics and hermeneutics on the design of open-air sound installations

According to Reybrouck (2004), *"The conceptual construction of time involves strategies of selection and semanticity"* (REYBROUCK, 2004:419). He points out that sound objects are temporal and that these objects can undergo variations in their extension of time, according to the symbol they represent. The author believes that the metaphorical relationship between sound and sign is a symbolic and empirical approach, which favours the mutuality of experience and conceptualization. Thus, by approaching musical ideas como temporals and in a symbolic way, it is possible to extend this metaphor to other musical parameters or ideas in order to optimize communication between those taking part in a show or concert.

Firstly, it is possible to observe the semantic load of the music and space relationship, where we look at: 1. the signs of the place of performance or exhibition; and 2. the signs present in the recordings. From another perspective, the semiotic content of the relationship between the soundscape present in the performance or exhibition environment and the intrinsic soundscape in the music is analyzed. Furthermore, the soundscape in recordings can naturally carry a dynamism and the notion of spatialization. In this way, it is possible to seek an association between the dynamics of the landscapes present in musical compositions and the dynamics of exhibition spaces.

Secondly, with regard to the dynamics of the spaces, I can see a first distinction between open and closed spaces: exhibitions in closed spaces, galleries and concert halls have very different acoustic, visual and cultural characteristics. We start from the premise that closed spaces delimit what will be perceived, keeping the receivers ideologically detached from the sound and visual content of the external environment; they contain a relative cultural heritage, where behavioral patterns are identified on the part of the receivers. In general, these places have the flexibility to form different performance spaces, where musical acoustics is one of the main parameters acting on the sound material. Thus, the acoustics of the room are the first conditioning factor. Likewise, the limitation of acoustic and visual information in the concert hall is a second constraint.

On the other hand, open spaces offer different types of dynamics, signs and are totally unpredictable - acoustically and visually. These phenomena, recognized functionally in the compositional act, would support the contextualization of listening. In this way, the open-air exhibition interferes significantly in the perception of the musical narrative, because the acoustic and visual reality of the exhibition space encourages the formation and transformation of the dynamics of the soundscape belonging to the musical composition. Based on the principle of mutuality, it is necessary to know how the phenomena of the exhibition space act on the narrative. Likewise, what other musical phenomena could be relevant to the perception of a work that integrates the acoustic and visual characteristics of the space.

Therefore, in order to help in this study of interpretation and in the construction of a concept that fosters a new discussion, Hermeneutics will help in the experience of exhibiting sound installations, based on the interpretation of the signs belonging to the recording spaces and the exhibition spaces. Initially, Gadamer (1964) presents the relationship between aesthetics and Hermeneutics. He points out that, *"In fact, there exists between the work and its respective observer an absolute simultaneity that remains unchallenged despite the growing lucidity of historical consciousness"* (GADAMER, 1964:01). Gadamer also points out that aesthetic consciousness can refer to the fact that the work of art has the potential to communicate itself, considering the conceptual inexhaustibility of artistic statements.

Based on Gadamer's Hermeneutics, a new hypothesis is created for the musical relationship between the use of the dynamics of performance spaces to support and supplement musical composition, from the use of their acoustic properties, to the appropriation of visual characteristics so that they can be integrated into the resulting concept of the work of art, optimizing communication and the multiple understanding of the vaguest musical phenomena. Thus, Gadamer (1964) points out: *"(...) it is no metaphor for the work of art that it tells us something and belongs as something that says something to the context of all that we have to understand"* (GADAMER, 1964:04). Therefore, by aiming for such communication that belongs to a context, musical interpretation gains hermeneutic support and criteria. In order to understand the sound installations, use is made of hermeneutic knowledge to verify which musical phenomena of compositional relevance are perceived in the exposition of the sound installations. Also, in what way are these musical phenomena accentuated by the context to which they are subjected.

To this end, Paul Ricoeur (2008) points out that

> *"Sensitivity to context* is the *necessary complement and inescapable counterpart of polysemy. But the handling of contexts, in turn, brings into play an activity of discernment which is exercised in the concrete exchange of messages between interlocutors, modeled on the game of question and answer. This activity of discernment is, in fact, interpretation: it consists of recognizing which relatively univocal message the speaker has constructed on the polysemous basis of the common lexicon. To produce a relatively univocal discourse with polysemous words, to identify this intention of univocity in the reception of messages, this is the first and most elementary work of interpretation" (RICOEUR, 2008:25).*

Thus, Gadamer points out that *"Every interpretation of something comprehensible, which helps others to reach comprehension, will certainly have a linguistic character"* (GADAMER, 1964:04). This quote takes us back to two other texts: Voice *and Language* (1981), by Gadamer, and *Semiotics and Philosophy of Language* (1984), by Umberto Eco. Firstly, because perception is the fundamental conditioning factor of musical existence, it is worth quoting Scheier for demonstrating that 'pure perception' is an abstraction from the context in which a work of art is inserted, based on the praise of the objectivity of perception.

> *"Pure" perception, "adequate to the stimuli",* is *an abstraction, so to speak - the point at which all orientation to the lived world disappears. Heidegger's great merit is to show that this abstraction relative to the full concretion of lived life is in fact one of the fundamental presuppositions of the 'objectivity' of scientific research, but contains behind it a passive ontological prejudice! to be glimpsed from the history of metaphysics"* (GADAMER, 1981:91).

On the other hand, it's also worth mentioning Kant's technical expression: the 'transcendental synthesis of perception'. In other words, Gadamer argues that the Kantian differentiation between 'substance' and 'subject' is fundamental to the real appropriation of knowledge by the perceiver. In this way, by moving through the statements of Scheier and Kant, Gadamer realizes that, *"From then on, all modern philosophy is marked by the reflexive structure of subjectivity"* (GADAMER, 1981:93). Therefore, providing musical listening that is integrated into the dynamic environment of open exhibition spaces is conceptually offering something that differs conceptually from what survives inertly in closed spaces. Likewise, by allowing these dynamics of the exhibition space to interfere in musical composition, sound diffusion and, consequently, musical perception, indeterminacy and musical subjectivity are widely accepted, whether conceptual or not.

Secondly, taking advantage of the unpredictability of the dynamics of the spaces, which is linked to musical subjectivity, it is essential to present new tools that support the perception of sound installations. In order to metaphorically associate the visual reality of the landscape contained in the exhibition spaces with the acoustic content made available, it is necessary to reflect on: symbol, ideogram, model, archetype, dream, desire, delirium, rite, myth, magic, creativity, paradigm, icon, representation, language, sign, meaning and sense. It is believed that this study would encourage the conceptualization of sound installations, aiming compositionally at the communicability and intelligibility of sound content.

According to Eco (1984), those who use metaphors in their discourse *"(...) speak obscurely and above all speak of something else, providing vague information"* (ECO, 1984:156). On the other hand, as Mitchell (1986) sees metaphor as a verbal representation of the image, it would become a convenient and useful tool for the musical experience. It requires meticulousness, a certain attention to how the musical content can allude to other references at the moment of composition and exhibition, compromising or optimizing the perception of the concept of a multimedia work.

Thus, by assuming that a sound installation exhibited in the open air can be understood as a multimedia work, the work of Santaella and Noth (1997) becomes indispensable, guiding the fields of: 1. the semiotics of the image; 2. the relationship between image/perception/time.

In this way, I would first like to emphasize the importance of the visual landscape combined with sound diffusion in a multimedia exhibition. In this case, a first hypothesis is to consider the images of the place as signs, both those of the exhibition space and those that may be being represented acoustically. Images, according to Santaella and Noth (1997), move between representation and imagination. For them,

> "The *concept of image is divided into a semantic field determined by two opposite poles. One describes the direct perceptual or even existing image. The other contains the simple mental image which, in the absence of visual stimuli, can be evoked"* (SANTAELLA and NOTH, 1997:38).

In this way, the 'semantic duality' of the division of the image into perception or imagination is presented.

Secondly, presenting Santaella and Noth's (1997) approach to the relationship between image, perception and time, the following phenomena are extracted: o intrinsic time, o extrinsic time and o interstitial time. As far as this study is concerned, I would highlight o interstitial time - o perception time. According to Santaella and Noth (1997),

> *"The adjective interstitial here qualifies the time that is born at the intersection between a perceiving subject and a perceived object, in other words, the time that is constructed in and by perception. At all levels, perception is made of time. Among the times of perception, the most important are o physiological time, o biological time and o logical time"* (SANTAELLA and NOTH, 1997:87).

At another point, we need to deepen our studies of this perceptive time, so that this musical phenomenon can be thought of compositionally with a view to the structural and diffusional malleability of a musical work. It is also necessary to foster new relationships between the concept of image and other musical phenomena, in order to further dissolve the boundaries between the visual field and the sound field.

Duhautpas and Solomos (2014) point out that the handle explores the soundscape, focusing on the acoustic specificities of the place. McCartney[7] (1999) also points out that

> *"The handle works to bring together the different sounds recorded in these forests: the sounds of running water, birds, flies, mosquitoes and mysterious sounds resulting from treatment in the studio"* (McCARNEY, 1999:344).

Thus, using the method of analysis developed by Voorvelt (1997) to analyze Barry Truax's compositional processes, this article will present the spatial aspects that involve the listener, such as the sounds that provide orientation points and the spatial movements that provide information about their sources.

The aim here is to present an overview, as well as to discuss the materials used to compose this work, relating them to the types of listening presented by Chion (2012). Thus, this work analyzes Westerkamp's work based on some paradigms of musical perception and semiotics, addressing: spatial aspects, acoustic perspective, complexity and symbolism.

7 "The piece operates on the encounter of different sounds recorded in these forests: sounds of running water, birds, flies, mosquitoes and mysterious sounds resulting from studio treatment (McCartney 1999, 344)."

## 4 Sound installation and spectromorphology

According to Denis Smalley, *"The spectromorphology approach establishes spectral and morphological models and processes, providing support for understanding the structural and behavioral relationships experienced in the temporal flow of music"* (SMALLEY, 1997:107). Thus, for Smalley, spectromorphology is not a compositional theory, but a tool for description based on auditory perception.

Therefore, spectromorphology was structured by Smalley as follows: 1. Definitions and contexts; 2. Gestures and their substitutes; 3. Spectromorphological expectations; 4. Gestures and textures сото forming principles; 5. Structural levels; 6. Structural fungi; 7. Movement and growing processes; 8. Textural movement; 9. Behavior; 10. Spectrum; 11. Spago and Spagomorphology. Thus, I will focus on the specific studies of behavior and spatial and spagomorphology, represented by items 9 and 11, respectively.

Firstly, Smalley defines that

> *"The metaphor of behavior is used to elaborate relationships between the various spectromorphologies that act in a musical context. I believe that listeners can intuitively diagnose behavioral relationships (or the lack thereof) in the context of electroacoustic music, and that these diagnoses affect listeners' interpretation of and reactions to the music"* (SMALLEY, 1997;117) .[8]

In this case, I will take as an example the main variants that exist in the exhibition of open-air sound installations: 1. the visual content; 2. the acoustic content of the place; and 3. the musical content. Firstly, following Fontana's example, it is known that the visual reality of the venue has an effect on the perception of the musical content. The study of spectromorphology points out that there are two opposing pairs of concepts that form part of the basis of the study of the interpretation of behavioral relationships: 1. dominance or subordination; and 2. conflict and coexistence.

8 "The metaphor of behavior is used to elaborate relationships among the variend spectromorpholofies acting within a musical context. I believe that listeners can intuitively diagnose behavioral relationships (or a lack of them) in electroacoustic music contexts and that this diagnosis affects the listener's interpretation of and reactions to the music" (SMALLEY, 1997:117).

From a study following the exhibition of my sound installation *'Spiritual Convergence',* I realized that, because I was using sounds from different sources, there was an intensified need to identify which musical parameters were dominant or subordinate to the acoustic content of the exhibition space. Also, to identify which musical parameters conflict or coexist with the visual content of the venue. Finally, this study would not delimit, but would expand the possibilities for integrating sound and space in the compositional process, from the process of transforming timbre to the planning of sound diffusion.

Secondly, with regard to space and its perception, Smalley (1997) defines that *"Spatial perception is inextricably bound up with spectromorphological content, and most listeners cannot easily appreciate ospace como an experience in itself"* (SMALLEY, 1997:122). He also points out that the term '*spatiomorphology'*

> *"(...) underlines this special concentration on the exploration of spatial properties and spatial changes, so that they constitute a different, yet separate category of sonic experience"* (SMALLEY, 1997:122) .[9]

Thus, to help develop compositional tools that support these concepts that integrate sound with the acoustic and visual qualities of the space, Smalley's ordering can be adopted as a first methodology, defining the six orientations that make up a global space.

9 "Spatial perception is inextricably bound up with spectromorphological content, and most listeners cannot easily appreciate space as an experience in itself. Spatial appreciation can be acquired by consciously listening to the spaces in works as distinct from regarding space only as spectromorphological enhancement. I use the term *spatiomorphology to* highlight this special concentration on exploring spatial properties and spatial change, such that they constitute a different, even separate category ofsonic experience" (SMALLEY, 1997:122).

## 5 Sound installation and psychoacoustics

When dealing with sound installations, it becomes relevant to also address the conditions of indoor spaces, presenting the reference that has already been built about room acoustics. As a justification for this work, I point out the reasons why I'm interested in integrating the acoustic and visual characteristics of exhibition spaces, primarily open-air ones.

Firstly, according to Fasti and Zwicker (2007), *"(...) room acoustics should also describe the conditions, leading to good listening in the room"* (FASTL and ZWICKER, 2OO7:366)[10] . The acoustic and visual particularities of both indoor and outdoor spaces have a unique dynamic that can promote the renewal of artistic-musical content. Knowing that the reception of artistic information is different for each type of space, it is necessary to try to understand how the acoustic and visual properties of internal spaces can contribute to the perception of the exhibition. In the future, the dynamics of external spaces can be considered an integral element of the structure, fundamental to the perception of the exhibition.

Secondly, Fasti and Zwicker (2007) point out that in order to optimize speech perception, some sound elements should be avoided in room acoustics. In this case, *"If the volumes of the 'echoes' are only one tenth of the initial value, the echoes should be ignored in speech perception"* (FASTL and ZWICKER, 2007:368)[11] . Certainly, сото о echo is a lower value and derived from a physically relevant initial value, in psychoacoustics it is considered irrelevant to speech perception. However, the phenomenon of 'echo' cannot be ignored in the view of semiotics, which understands the possible network of meanings that is created by admitting that echo is an element that transforms the sound object belonging to the composition of the work of art.

Finally, exposure to external spaces increases compositional uncertainties, offering a wealth of information that can be predicted, but not easily manipulated or ignored. Clearly,

---

10 "Room acoustics uses mostly physical values. However, room acoustics should also describe the conditions leading to good hearing in a room. Because hearing characteristics are described by psychoacoustical data and values, it seems reasonable to introduce these values into the description of room acoustics" (FASTL and ZWICKER, 2007:366).
11 "If the loudness of the echos is only a tenth of the initial value, the echos may be ignored in speech perception" (FASTL and ZWICKER, 2007:368).

this information can be approached in countless ways in a compositional process, and this sound content of the space can form part of the structure of the sound installation. Thus, it is worth debating whether this improbability can be accepted structurally, understanding that this indeterminacy is part of the subjectivity envisaged in the compositional act. This will intensify the possibilities of discussing a new possibility of an open work.

## 6 Sound installation and Soundwalk

The use of *soundwalkscomo* compositional sound material

Following the thought of spatial morphology, I propose the use of '*soundwalks*' in the composition of sound installations, for the conceptual redefinition of the 'spatialization' of musical materials, and for the adoption of an 'expanded field of diffusion' .[12]

Firstly, *'Soundwalk'* was defined by Westerkamp as a method that incorporates a personal connection with the soundscape through focused listening during a walk. Poll! (2011) points out that the main purpose of a '*Soundwalk*' is to listen to the soundscape of an environment. He also points out that *soundwalking* allows you to engage with the soundscape, which can be related to political and social issues. Polli points out that

> "*Soundwalks* and soundscape composition can serve as a philosophical and political practice, where these interdisciplinary practices can create paths for the development of knowledge from a personal, environmental and political perspective" (POLLI, 2011:259) .[13]

Polli (2011) concludes that "The *soundwalk, by its nature, is a subjective experience, and the structure of soundwalk compositions emphasizes this subjectivity** (POLLI, 2011:267)[14] . In this way, since my compositional processes are governed by indeterminacies, dubieties, metaphors and allusions, it wouldn't be out of place to appropriate tools that would offer my composition a new dynamic, which would be engaged with the dynamics of the spaces contained in each recording.

Secondly, because I believe that composing with environmental sounds keeps the listener attentive to a peculiar and subjective narrative component - the visuality of the space - I believe that it is also possible to understand it as a first-person soundscape when movement is attributed to the observer. In other words, the *sound* content of the *soundwalk* enables the listener to become more integrated with the narrative on display and the elements belonging to the exhibition spaces. Thus, the concept of sound diffusion should also be expanded in order to expand, optimize and resignify the perception of the content

12 A term that arises from the relationship between sound diffusion and expanded cinema. Expanded cinema offers new possibilities for image diffusion, antagonistic to the narrative-representative-industrial model.
13 "Soundwalking and soundscape composition can serve as both a philosophical and political practice, and these interdisciplinary practices can create alternative pathways for increasing environmental knowing from a personal environmental and political perspective" (POLLI, 2011:259).
14 "Soundwalking by its nature is a subjective experience, and the structure of soundwalking compositions emphasizes this subjectivity" (POLLI, 2011:267).

being exhibited.

Finally, this visuality of the space and the reception of the content of the recordings can immediately refer to the receiver's personal relationship with the visual and acoustic reality of the exhibition spaces. Based on this, I think it's essential to see how the use of *soundwalks* can be approached artistically, in musical composition and exhibition.

## Soundscape in the work of Hildegard Westerkamp

Hildegard Westerkamp was a pioneer of ecological acoustics. For the composition of the work, Westerkamp recorded sounds from the landscape of *Carmanah Valley (figure 1),* on Vancouver Island, but also in forests near *Cowichan Lake (figure 2),* tai сото on Galeano Island and in *Lighthouse Park,* places close to Vancouver. According to Duhautpas and Solomos[15] (2014), music can be understood as an experience and, in particular, as an experience of place. In this way, it is pointed out that the work was "Composed from sounds recorded in an ancient forest located on the West Coast of British Columbia, this handle directs us through a visible forest (...)" (Duhautpas and Solomos, 2014:06).

*Figure 1: Carmanah Valley. Extracted from the internet on June 28, 2017.*

15 "(...) music as experience and, in particular, as experience of place(...)" (Duhautpas and Solomos, 2014:06).

*Figure 2: Cowichan Lake. Extracted from the internet on June 28, 2017.*

Duhautpas and Solomos (2014) point out that the handle explores the soundscape, focusing on the acoustic specificities of the place. McCartney[16] (1999) also points out that

> *"The handle works to bring together the different sounds recorded in these forests: the sounds of running water, birds, flies, mosquitoes and mysterious sounds resulting from treatment in the studio"* (McCARNEY, 1999:344).

Thus, using the method of analysis developed by Voorvelt (1997) to analyze Barry Truax's compositional processes, the spatial aspects that involve the listener will be presented, such as the sounds that provide orientation points and the spatial movements that provide information about their sources.

## Overall view of the work

'Soundscape' is a term defined by the Canadian composer R. Murray Schafer who, according to Polli (2011), o makes an analogy with the visual landscape of a specific place. Thus, soundscape composition contains the sounds of the environment, portraying a

16 "The piece operates on the encounter ofdifferent sounds recorded in these forests: sounds of running water, birds, flies, mosquitoes and mysterious sounds resulting from studio treatment (McCartney 1999, 344)."

specific landscape or creating an imaginary environment. Deery (2015) defines the concept of soundscape composition as a natural progression of ecological acoustics and soundscape studies. It is well known that these studies were part of a global movement called the *World Soundscape Project,* founded in the 1980s by a community of artists, activists and scientists. The main names belonging to this group were: Barry Truax, Howard Bloomfield, Peter Huse, Bruce Davis and Hildegard Westerkamp.

According to Voorvelt[17] (1997), the group's aim was to study environmental sounds and their psychological and social effects. Voorvelt (1997) also presents the first conclusions of this group's work, where it was defined that "*environmental noise should not be viewed negatively, in an* exclusionary *way*"[18] (VOORVELT, 1997:49). Likewise, Voorvelt determines two given relationships between music and acoustic design: music in the soundscape and soundscape in music. Music in the soundscape comprises *"(...) compositions that are understood as alternative soundscapes, which must be integrated into the listener's acoustic environment"* (VOORVELT, 1997:50)[19] . The soundscape in music, on the other hand, is a less obvious relationship in which spatial aspects are involved; the acoustic perspective; the connection with the sounds of the landscape; and the relationship with symbolism.[20]

Schafer also (1977) categorizes music, defining that *"Music can belong to two species: absolute and programmatic"* (SCHAFER, 1977:151). He defines programmatic music as music that imitates the environment and can be paraphrased verbally in the concert program. Absolute music - which is not related to the work under discussion - is detached from the external environment and its forms are designed to be performed only in concert halls. In this case, for the work *"Beneath the Florest Floor"* (1992), by Westerkamp (1946), the soundscape is defined as representative and descriptive, pointing to characteristics of programmatic music.

Furthermore, the sounds precisely determine the environment in which they were recorded, as the materials belonging to the composition have the function of accurately portraying a

17 "(...) environmental sounds and their psychoological and sociological effects" (VOORVELT, 1997:49).
18 "One of the Project's first conclusions was that noise pollution should not be fought in a negative, excluding way(...)" (VOORVELT, 1997:49).
19 "Here, compositions are understood as alternative soundscapes, which should be integrated in the listener's acoustic environment" (VOORVELT, 1997:50).
20 See (VOORVELT, 1997:51-53).

specific environment. In short, a non-oral musical discourse is separated into two pianos, presenting the elements of the Canadian soundscape. This landscape is presented in a fragmented way, where the musical fragments are of short duration, intersected by a continuous and percussive sound. Similarly, McCartney (1999) defines the magpie which, overall, consists of a heavy, deep sound that regularly returns to a percussive marking to punctuate the magpie. Therefore, the sounds that refer to a specific soundscape are interwoven. These sounds, which are literal representations of the soundscape, are then gradually processed and re-presented.

However, in *'Beneath the Florest Floor'* (1992), urban noise is not used in the compositional process, as only the natural sounds of the Canadian forest are used. Based on these materials and the electroacoustic treatment given to them, this work is considered a soundscape composition. Deery[21] (2015) points out that the concept of soundscape composition occurs como a natural progression from acoustic ecology and soundscape studies, where the *"soundscape is considered como a vast musical composition, unfolding around us, ceaselessly"* (DEERY cit. SCHAFER, 2015:33). In other words, Deery defines a soundscape as a narrative full of meaning that builds mental images, helping us to recognize an environment that is formed or represented.

Schafer (1977) states that *"Every natural soundscape has its own peculiar sound, and often these sounds are so original that they constitute sonic landmarks"* (SCHAFER, 1977:48). In Westerkamp's work, the sounds determine precisely the environment in which they were recorded, since the materials belonging to the composition have the function of accurately portraying a specific environment. Thus, in a non-oral musical discourse separated into two pianos, the elements of the Canadian soundscape are presented. This landscape is presented in a fragmented way, where the musical fragments are of short duration, intersected by a continuous and percussive sound. Similarly, McCartney (1999) defines the magpie which, overall, consists of a heavy, deep sound that regularly returns to a percussive marking to punctuate the magpie. Therefore, the sounds that refer to a specific soundscape are interwoven. These sounds, which are literal representations of the soundscape, are then gradually processed and re-presented.

21 "The conception of soundscape composition as a natural progression of acoustic ecology and soundscape studies owes much to concept that the soundscape - or sonic environment - is considered as a 'vast musical composition unfolding around us ceaselessly'" (DEERY cit. SCHAFER, 2015:33).

## Sound materials

The different complexities of sound - which are found in different parts of the world - precisely define the peculiarities of each place. The sounds of birds, the swaying of leaves and tree branches in the wind, the sound of flowing water or a storm all contribute to the formation of mental images and the creation of an imaginary space. As an example, Schafer was struck by the richness of sound in Tikitere, New Zealand. He defines the place as "a festering sore on the skin of the earth, with internal boiling sound effects spreading with the winds" (SCHAFER, 1977:48). Unlike the hostile environment presented by Schafer, Westerkamp offers a kind of 'sound garden'[22] , in which

> *"A sound garden is a place where nature is cultivated. It is a humanized treatment of the landscape. Trees, fruit, flowers, grass are organically sculpted into the wild vegetation by art and science. Sometimes the garden is drastically cut and "manicured", as in the rigidly classical gardens of Versailles and Vienna. Elsewhere, man has limited himself to promoting the flowering of certain structures characteristic of the landscape"* (SCHAFER, 1977:341).

Thus, in using the materials of the space, Westerkamp recreates specific places in a landscape. With reference to water - an important sound object used by Westerkamp in the construction of the work - Schafer (1977) had defined that

> *"It was in the Italian gardens of the Renaissance and Baroque that water was given a special character of elegance and beauty, as its freshness provided a delicious contrast to the extreme brightness of the hot summer"* (SCHAFER, 1977:343).

In the work, Westerkamp clearly defines the soundscape, literally using the materials that served as the basis for the composition. By preserving the intelligibility of the sound source in the materials belonging to the landscape, she preserves its expressiveness and also the intrinsic meanings of each material. She also preserves the 'eloquence of water'[23] , keeping it ever-present in her compositional process. Westerkamp uses spatialization to highlight the movement of water, where it flows in the same direction, from left to right, in a *pan* effect. Where there is some variation in this direction of movement, an alteration or displacement can be defined by a pseudo-observer, who points out other perspectives for perceiving the same soundscape.

As well as water, the sounds of birds are constantly present in Westerkamp's soundscape. Schafer (1977) points out that "Every territory on Earth will have its own symphony of birds,

22 A term used and defined by Schafer in his book "The Tuning of the World".
23 A term used and defined by Schafer in his book "The Tuning of the World".

producing a fundamental native sound - as characteristic as the language of the men who live there" (SCHAFER, 1977:56). Schafer (1977) also emphasizes the importance of birdsong. According to him, not only do birds historically contribute to the feeling of happiness in a garden, but it is in birdsong that *"(...) we find the genesis of the idea of acoustic space"* (SCHAFER, 1977:58). Westerkamp uses the sounds of different birds in his work. From the recording and the treatment given to the materials, the composer changes perspectives by making details contained in the sound explicit and by using the *pan* effect *(04'51"),* which translates into movement and designs the acoustic space. According to Schafer (1977),

> *"The definition of space by meanings is much older than the establishment of fences and property boundaries; and as private property becomes more and more threatening in the modern world, it is to be believed that the principles regulating the complex network of acoustic spaces that overlap and interpenetrate, como occur between birds and animals, will once again have great significance for the human community as well"*
> (SCHAFER, 1977:58).

To create the soundscape in its entirety, Westerkamp uses insect sounds *(02' 28" - 03' 05")* to complement the soundscape. These complex sounds are also presented clearly, without any apparent electronic intervention. According to Schafer (1977), knowing that the common bee produces a sound of approximately 200 to 250 cycles per second, he defines these frequencies "as the basic notes of the resulting sounds; but, coто a rich spectrum of harmonics is always present, o the result can be a mixed sound, coто a barely discernible tuning fork" (SCHAFER, 1977:60). By preserving the intelligibility of the source of the sound material produced by the insects, the idea of the movement they produce has been maintained, preserving the dynamics of Westerkamp's soundscape.

Finally, Westerkamp presents the entire sound space at the end of the work (12' 06"). Leppert (2012) points out that *"The forest is a privileged space, both legally and symbolically"*[24] (LEPPERT, 2012:413). Knowing the importance of constructing a symbol in order to sustain the intelligibility and communication of the discourse, I quote Eco (1984) who had already pointed out that *"(...) all truly rigorous and exact thought only finds its firm point in the symbolism, in the semiotics, on which it rests"* (ECO, 1984:222). Thus, Duhautpas and Solomos (2014) point out that the interaction between the different sounds used in the magpie contributes to creating an atmosphere of peace, mystery, the eternal and the unreal.

24 "The forest is a privileged space, both legally and symbolically" (LEPPERT, 2012:413).

## 7 The sound installation *'SPIRITUAL CONVERGENCE'* (2014)

Some questions about time and space in music arose after the performance of the sound installation called *'Spiritual Convergence',* composed in 2014 and exhibited at the Autonomous University of Madrid. The sound installation, which was presented in an open space with a flow of people, made it possible to create a new sense of space and time, offering a new possibility of dialogue with the exhibition spaces, where acoustic and visual aspects were observed that contributed to the conceptualization of the work.

*Figure 1: Autonomous University of Madrid. Photograph by the author. Madrid, 2014.*

Specifically, this sound installation was conceived coто a handle with a malleable format, built from autonomous handles approached coто events, which can be enlarged or reduced. In addition to the possibility of being exhibited in the open air, galleries or concert halls, the redefinition of the time of the events present in the sound installation makes it possible to preserve its formal structure and therefore preserve the characteristics of the narrative structure. What's more, it's the organization into events that generates the malleability of its structure, allowing the concept of the work to survive when presented in different places.

Two points were fundamental to the construction of the sound installation: 1. the degree of coherence in the development of the narrative of each musical piece; and 2. the cohesion between the pieces. As an example, I present two tracks that are part of the sound installation *'Spiritual Convergence',* named separately: *'Spiritual Convergence'* and *'Cold Place'.* Firstly, the tracks *'Spiritual Convergence'* and *'Cold Place'* were composed using instrumental improvisation. The improvisation essentially used the *Persian* flute *(Persian Ney)* and a set of Tibetan tags. The recording was made by sectioning the improvisation into events, conceiving in advance the electroacoustic music procedures to which the recordings would be subjected. Thus, the materials were catalogued for the construction of the musical narrative, using сото o *delay* and o *reverb* resources, essentially.

*Figure 2: O flow of people in the space. Photograph by the author. Madrid, 2014.*

Secondly, it's worth noting the use of sounds from the soundscape in the *'Cold Place' piece,* where the sounds of rain and thunderstorms can be easily identified. In this case, the relationship between creative processes and the environment also stands out. Numerous art forms have been studied, structured and presented in open spaces, galleries or concert halls. According to Mohr (2007), contemporary culture is basically visual. Therefore, try to contextualize the materials from instrumental recording with the use of soundscape material. In addition, presenting musical material that represents rain and exposing it to the open air would, in my opinion, provide a greater range of physical experience due to the visuality in the perception process, where, according to Mohr, the listening participants would be more engaged with the environment and the perceptual relationships it can produce.

Thus, with regard to the use of soundscape materials in musical composition, Truax (1996) concluded that

> "The *principles of soundscape composition are: 1. recognition by the listener when the sound source material is retained, even if it is subsequently subjected to transformation; 2. the listener's knowledge of the environmental and psychological context of the material is invoked and encouraged to complete the network of meanings assigned to the music; 3. The composer's knowledge of the psychological and environmental context of the soundscape material allows them to influence the form of the composition at each level and, ultimately, the composition is inseparable from some or all of its aspects of reality; and ideally, 4. It is the work of our understanding of the world and its influences that are brought into everyday perceptual habits*" (TRUAX, 1996:63) .[25]

In this way, I approached the process of composing the '*Cold Place*' piece as an integrated process of listening and visuality, with a view to recontextualizing the musical materials when the installation is exposed to the open air. In this way, a new psychological and environmental context was created to complement and compose new networks of meanings for the recorded musical materials.

25 "The principles ofthe soundscape composition are: (a) listener recognizability ofthe source material is maintained, even if it subsequently undergoes transformation; (b) the listener's knowledge of the environmental and psychological context of the soundscape material is invoked and encouraged to complete the network of meanings ascribed to the music; (c) the composer's knowledge ofthe environmental and psychological context ofthe soundscape material is allowed to influence the shape ofthe composition at every level, and ultimately the composition is inseparable from some or all ofthose aspects of reality; and ideally, (d) the work enhances our understanding ofthe world, and its influence carries over into everyday perceptual habits"(TRUAX, 1996:63).

*Figure 3: The sound devices. Photograph by the author. Madrid, 2014.*

Similarly, Fontana (1987) previously sought to recontextualize the sounds of the environment, relocating the sounds belonging to a given environment in another, so that it would be possible to redefine them. Fontana (1987:154) points out that he conceived of these relocations in sculptural terms:

> *"I conceived of such relocations in sculptural terms because ambient sounds are sculptural in the sense that they belong to a specific place. To make art out of an ambient sound, the act of placing the sound must have considerable aesthetic importance"* (FONTANA, 1987:154) .[26]

Knowing that *"(...) sounds are not isolated from their contexts"* (FONTANA, 1987:154)[27] , it becomes possible to use the materials of the soundscape considering this performative procedure сото a possible tool that makes it possible to highlight the signs belonging to each place of exhibition from the compositional process, favoring integration and communication in the musical environment, primarily in open spaces.

26 "I conceived such relocations in sculptural terms because ambient sounds are sculptural in the way they belong to a particular place. To make art out of an ambient sound, the act of placing this sound would have considerable aesthetic importance" (FONTANA, 1987:154).
27 "In both my field recording and sound sculpture, sounds are not isolated from their contexts; in relocating sounds, I have been concerned with the contexts in which the sounds are placed and with the sculptural/spatial qualities ofthe sound source" (FONTANA, 1987:154).

In this way, Fontana (1987) describes three works that illustrate the repositioning of sounds from the recording environment in a new performative environmental context: 1. *Oscillating Steel Grids Along the Brooklyn Bridge; 2.Entfernte Zuge (Distant Trains);* and 3. *Metropolis Koln.* Essentially, I would like to highlight the main characteristic of the work *"Metropolis Koln".* Fontana (1987) points out that he was concerned with the perceived scale of the sound source, manipulating its meaning by juxtaposing the sound with the physical or architectural elements of the exhibition site. This procedure, which took place in September 1985, was unconsciously repeated by me in 2014 at the *"Espartos Sonoros 2014"* congress in Madrid, where the sound diffusion equipment that conditioned the exhibition allowed the acoustic qualities of the space to be observed in order to optimize the exhibition.

Having presented some of Fontana's compositional procedures and concepts that have been used to recontextualize and integrate sound material when associated with a new spatial reality, it is important to delve deeper into the agents that interfere with the perception of a sound installation when exposed to the open air. First and foremost, the aim is to create compositional tools that support the dialog between sound and visual and acoustic phenomena belonging to different types of environment, either with the support of the aforementioned studies of Semiotics and Hermeneutics, or with the support of Spectromorphology or Psychoacoustics.

## The sound installation *'SAVING SHAPES' (2017)*

A first motivation for starting a long and continuous process of living in a particular space was Heidegger's well-known appropriation of the Todtnauberg space for his intellectual and philosophical development, in parallel with the academic environment. Sharr (2009) points out that for Heidegger's philosophical production, nature and its movements were sonorous and essential. O environment endowed with sound and a unique view exerted a strong influence on the philosopher's creation, where he "(...) submitted himself to the rhythms and connections of the landscape (...)" (SHARR, 2009:73)[28] . Reflecting on the importance that space had for Heidegger's intellectual production, I was driven to realize moments of sound reception in a specific landscape - this one inhospitable and with noises

28 "(...) to subject oneself to the rhythms and lessons of the landscape, there was always somewhere a parallel life of human interests" (SHARR, 2009:73).

characteristic of the environment, where compositional and installation practice is full of instability and indeterminacy.

O sound recording

According to Schafer (1977), the different complexities of sound found in different parts of the world precisely define the peculiarities of each place. The sounds of birds, the swaying of leaves and tree branches in the wind, the sound of flowing water, a storm, or even the sounds of cars and the movement of the urban landscape all contribute to the formation of mental images and the creation of an imaginary space. For example, Schafer was impressed by the richness of sound in Tikitere, New Zealand. He defines the place as "*(...) a pustulent sore on the floor of the earth, with boiling internal sound effects spreading with the winds*" (SCHAFER, 1977:48). Unlike this hostile environment presented by Schafer, Westerkamp offers in his work *'Beneath the Florest Floor'* (1996) a kind of 'sound garden'[29] , in which

> *"A sound garden is a place where nature is cultivated. It is a humanized treatment of the landscape. Trees, fruit, flowers, grass are organically sculpted into the wild vegetation by art and science. Sometimes the garden is drastically cut and "manicured", as in the rigidly classical gardens of Versailles and Vienna. Elsewhere, man limited himself to promoting the flowering of certain structures characteristic of the landscape" (SCHAFER. 1977:341).*

Thus, I use recording processes in the same space at different times of the year, looking at the sonic transformation of the place and, consequently, the transformation of the sound recording and musical composition. With regard to the soundscape recording process, Voorvelt (1997) points out that

> *"Recording and sampling have many consequences for the aesthetics of music, even though music is no longer a purely abstract language of human construction, it can now include existing sounds that contain various kinds of connotation" (VOORVELT, 1997:48) .*[30]

As this is an installation composed to be presented in the open air, all compositional, installation and receptive practice is completely conditioned by these innumerable factors of instability and indeterminacy. These are: 1. dynamic factors that alter the sounds of the landscape; 2. human interventions; 3. signs of human traffic and depredation; and 4. transformations of the landscape over the course of the day, the seasons and the years.

29 A term used and defined by Schafer in his book "The Tuning of the World".
30 "Recording and sampling has many consequences for the aesthetics of music, since music is no longer an abstract language of purely human construction, but can now include pre-existing sounds that carry all kinds of connotations" (VOORVELT, 1997:48).

*Figure 4: O sound recording device. Photograph by the author. Ilha dos Marinheiros, March 2017.*

According to Voorvelt (1997), Truax calls his electroacoustic works 'sound environments', where he suggests that the listener's experience is linked to their own sense of space and the qualities of the space to which they belong, subverting the traditional listening experience into a broad perceptual field. Voorvelt (1997) points out that the *"(...) characteristics of the soundscape define the sound environment"* (VOORVELT, 1997:51)[31] . In this case, the characteristics of the sound environment pointed out by Voorvelt (1997) are: 1. O spatial aspect; 2. acoustic perspective; 3. acoustic functions; 4. complexity; and 5. O symbolism.

Firstly, o *spatial aspect* and presented according to Voorvelt (1997) coтo

> *"An environment typically surrounds the listener, while sounds provide orientation points. Thus, spatial movements provide information about their sources" (VOORVELT, 1997:51).*

Secondly, the *acoustic perspective* is considered. According to Voorvelt, Schafer and Truax, *"The research of the World Soundscape Project has suggested that natural sounds owe their meanings and effects in part to their place, numa hierarchy of layers".*

31 "Such soundscape-characteristics define the sonic environment" (VOORVELT, 1997:51).

(VOORVELT, 1997:52). Furthermore, "*According to Schafer and Truax, a healthy acoustic ecosystem is characterized (among other things) by a balanced relationship between first and second piano*" (VOORVELT, 1997:52).

Thirdly, Voorvelt (1997) summarizes the *acoustic functions*: 1. *'keynote sounds'* - sounds considered to be second piano sounds that form an integral part of the landscape; 2. *'signals'* - sounds considered to be first piano sounds, presented clearly and that directly capture the listener's attention; 3. *'soundmarks'* - sounds that have a social function, сото о the sound of church bells; 4. *'archetypal* sounds' - sounds that have a symbolic association. Fourthly, Voorvelt (1997) organizes complexity into different areas: 1. *"many natural sounds are stochastically organized"* (VOORVELT, 1997:52);[32] 2 . *"landscape sounds possess timbral complexity"* (VOORVELT, 1997:52)[33] ; and 3. *"every natural sound will be associated with a particular sound source and its known connotations"* (VOORVELT, 1997:53)[34] . Finally, symbolism is directly connected to the complexity and acoustic function of sound. These categorizations will help in the understanding, analysis and sound composition of real and coherent ecosystems.

## Characteristics of the Soundscape

The sound installation *'Saving Shapes'* has four different moments in its exhibition, in which contrasts are sought between the parts, both acoustically and visually. One of the questions that arose from the soundwalks in that landscape was how the weather interfered with the recording, planning, composition and presentation. Firstly, the transformations in the landscape caused by climate change were extremely important for the composition of the track. During the walks in the summer months of 2016/2017, from December 21 to March 20, intense landscape transformations were identified, where flooding was caused by rain falling on sandy soil. Secondly, in terms of human interference in the performance space, there were signs of the native vegetation of the dunes being set on fire, as well as the burning of trees that existed there and which would certainly have been the habitat of other species that made up the soundscape of this space.

32 "many natural sounds are organized stochastically (...)" (VOORVELT, 1997:52).
33 "environmental sounds have a timbral complexity, (...)" (VOORVELT, 1997:52)
34 "every natural sound will be associated with a particular sound source and related connotations, (...) (VOORVELT, 1997:52).

*Figure 5: Presentation space. Ilha dos Marinheiros, March 12, 2017.*

The transformation of the performance space during the seasons is the main factor behind the construction of a long-term exhibition. The changes to the landscape were considered, from its visual characteristics to its acoustic characteristics, from the process of recording the soundwalks to the installation processes. However, the transformations caused by human interference are too abrupt, where they are immediately identifiable, both visibly and acoustically. Such interventions in the soundscape alter and encourage compositional decisions, also stemming from these instabilities and uncertainties that the open space of presentation provides.

The seasons and their contrasts heighten the sense of instability and uncertainty of the space's behavior during the exhibition period. I was therefore interested in the fact that the entire construction of this installation process was based on conditioning the compositional process and the installation process to the transformations of the presentation space. Also, that the processes were built with the support of the unknown and the indeterminate, where chance is present and always pertinent to the construction of the installation work.

*Figure 6: Presentation space. Ilha dos Marinheiros, March 12, 2017.*

It should be emphasized that the identification of variations in the visual elements of the presentation landscape are just as relevant to communication as the transformation of the acoustic elements of the landscape. These variations affect the recording of the *soundwalks,* the duration of the sound installation and the positioning of the emitting devices. Finally, figure 2 shows the space adopted for the presentation on April 22, 2017.

*Figure 7: Presentation space. Ilha dos Marinheiros, April 22, 2017.*

## Communication in the presentation environment

Barry Truax (1984) points out a series of elements that make up acoustic communication, referring to the study of the soundscape. I would like to highlight the so-called '*keynote sounds*' that make up a soundscape. According to Truax (1984), 'keynote sounds' are an analogy to tonal music, which in the context of the soundscape, "*(...) are part of the ambience, at a low and constant level, such as an electric buzz or distant traffic; (...) a sound that remains outside the landscape and is clearly distinguishable from the ambient noise*" (TRUAX, 1984:22)[35] . In this way, the work *"Saving Shapes"* was composed with sounds from the environment to which it will be presented, avoiding in the recordings the possible interference of sounds that are not part of this particular acoustic and visual context.

35 "(...) may be part of the ambience, i.e., at a low, constant level, such as electrical hum or distant traffic; but it may also be a sound signal, i.e., a sound that stands out in an environment and is clearly distinguishable from the ambient noise. Examples of the latter type of keynote would be the sound of an ambulance siren near a busy hospital, the sound of train whistles to nearby residents, or the regular ringing of bells at fixed time intervals, as often occurs in European communities" (TRUAX, 1984:22).

*Figure 8: Presentation space: panoramic view. Ilha dos Marinheiros, March 12, 2017.*

As far as the structure of the work is concerned, this composition was created for a specific place and is organized by short sound structures that enable integration with the sounds of the soundscape itself. The intention is to make it possible to form a macro-structure, considerably integrating the sounds that have been recorded, edited and displayed in the presentation space. To this end, the sound recordings of the *soundwalks* are the basis for the electroacoustic composition of the sound installation, where geophonic, biophonic and anthropophonic elements will be recorded over a period of one year, adopting their variations over this period as fundamental to the transformation of the work over time.

*Figure 9: Presentation Space: panoramic view. Ilha dos Marinheiros, April 22, 2017.*

LaBelle (2006) had pointed out that Max Neuhaus held open-air exhibitions and thus caused the formation of seven different small spaces, characterized by different radio transmitter noises. However, even though the frequencies of the radios emitted are different, there is a similar concept in each space and a sound that constitutes a homogeneous whole. The question arises as to what possible consequences or effects the change of presentation space would have on the structure of the composer's work. Furthermore, the use of 7 different listening points establishes alternatives to the sound diffusion precepts of electroacoustic music in concert halls.

*Figure 10: Presentation space: local view. Ilha dos Marinheiros, April 22, 2017.*

As for the importance of communication in this artistic process, the precepts of variation and coherence will be the main points of departure and construction of a long exhibition work. Firstly, Truax (1985) points out that "the basic unit of information can be traced back to the perception of a "difference" - a comparison that discovers change between the current state of the environment and previous states" (TRUAX, 1984:100)[36] . On the other hand,

> *"The various trends in contemporary music, too numerous to describe here, can be understood como explore particular ways of maintaining musical coherence in the face of "free" combination and design of sound material"* (TRUAX, 1984:102) .[37]

In other words, there are countless possibilities for obtaining variations in sound material that make it possible to achieve coherence in a sound-music construction process. According to Truax (1984),

> *"From this cursory look at some of the acoustic design features of music, it can be seen that they all represent techniques for achieving coherence while allowing for variety, or more simply,*

36 "The basic unit of information itself can be traced to the perception of a "difference"-a comparison that discovers change between the present state of the environment and previous states" (TRUAX, 1984:100).
37 "The various trends in contemporary music, far too numerous to be described here, can be understood as exploring particular ways in which musical coherence may be maintained in the face ofthe "free" combination and design ofsound material" (TRUAX, 1984:102).

*for organizing information numa meaningful communication"* (TRUAX, 1984:102) .[38]

In this way, I tried to structure a recording process that, from the outset, established a process of variation and coherence. Thus, Barry Truax's (2012) practice suggestion indicated to me that one of the main acts of musical composition will be *soundwalks.* This act will provide the composer with the recognition of sound and aesthetic possibilities so that the artistic production in the space is coherent, while also analyzing new resources for its variation over time. In short, the massive repetition of this process proposes an intense relationship between composer and space, aimed at an intimate relationship of exploration and dialogue.

*Figure 11: Presentation Space: local view. Ilha dos Marinheiros, December 2004.*

From a practical perspective, *soundwalks* offer improvisational character, movement, path, transformation and coherence to the compositional process. First of all, improvisation with objects belonging to the place will help in the elaboration of new sound materials, thus

38 "From this cursory overview of some of the acoustic design features of music, it can be seen that all of them represent techniques for achieving coherence while permitting variety, or more simply, for organizing information into meaningful communication" (TRUAX, 1984:102).

supporting listeners in listening to the space that surrounds them. The movement facilitates the identification of a narrator, a being who observes the landscape and constructs an auditory and visual path, a kind of guide for listening and who guides the transformation and the process of reception in a coherent way.

Transposing the work's macro-structure to us, it is a long composition presented in an open space in constant transformation. Thus, the composition provides the means to overcome the need for repetition of sound material. In order to do this, it became necessary to plan a sequence of presentations and elaborate a cyclical process of sound recording, composition and installation, following a process that establishes contrasts while at the same time presenting coherence by varying the same sound source. The contrast and sequence of events to which I refer occurs through cumulative processes of transformation of the same sound material. The insertion of new sound elements establishes new dynamics in the compositional environment, where the role of each sound material changes throughout the compositional process. As one of the main structuring elements, the performance space acts constantly, acoustically and visually. It acts intensely at the intersections, periods in which the electroacoustic piano is inactive in the performance.

*Figure 12: Presentation Space. Ilha dos Marinheiros, December 2004. Photograph by the author.*

## Sound diffusion plan and sculpture in the landscape

O planning the sound diffusion of the work "*Saving Shapes*" intends to reflect on: 1. the technical part for the open-air sound installation; 2. the concealment or presentation of the emitting device; 3. the exploitation of the acoustics and objects of the space; 4. the organization of the macro-structure based on the climatic and logistical conditions of the space; 5. the time of the presentation; and 6. the approach or contrast generated by the sound installation. the organization of the macro-structure based on the climatic and logistical conditions of the performance space; 5. the performance schedule; and 6. the approximation or contrast generated between the electroacoustic piano and the natural piano in the landscape. It also aims to present which devices were used for sound diffusion, discussing the use of different loudspeakers in the conception of the work, from the sonic detail to the visual effect of the device on the listeners' reception.

## 8 Installing the devices

Antunes Pires (2007) points out the importance of interpreting the sound space before installing the device. According to her, *"The very idea of the most common physical space about the musical field is really o place spreading o sound - projection, rather than ways of working como physical phenomena unfolded in a particular place and at a definite point in time"* (ANTUNES PIRES, 2007:142)[39] . The author also considers the multiplicity of systems and the disparity of results when identical systems are used in different spaces: *"Thinking only of public concert situations, we will see the multiplicity of systems and the disparity that sometimes exists when installing the same system in two different listening locations"* (ANTUNES PIRES, 2007:142) . [40]

Finally, she discusses the role of the sound device in a work, where "... the *problems associated with projection devices are not just simple interactions between the device, its installation, the work and the projection site. We can see this in the fact that, at times, some systems have proved to be unsuitable for certain works"* (ANTUNES PIRES, 2007:142) .[41]

Thus, the first performance of the sound installation *'Saving Shapes'* (2017) took place on Saturday afternoon, April 22, 2017. For this first performance, 8 speakers, 1 amplifier and 200 meters of wire were used to connect the speakers. The diffusion was planned so that four private listening points were organized to form a shared listening space. This is due to the positioning of the speakers; because the presentation space is large; and because the sound diffusion system is low-powered. An analogy to listening with headphones, where Antunes Pires (2007) points out that *"Duchenne believes that listening using headphones '(...) represents a very interesting variant of listening at home (...) due to the individualization of the external area created* (ANTUNES PIRES, 2007:152)[42] . The following figure shows the devices that were used in the first performance and how they were placed in the space:

---

39 "L'idee meme d'espace physique la plus commune en ce qui concerne le champ musical est effectivement celle de lieu d'etalement du sonore, de lieu de projection des formes de l'oeuvre en tant que phenomenes physiques deplies dans un endroit determin et a un momenti defini du temps" (ANTUNES PIRES, 2007:137).
40 "Reflecting only on public concert situations, we can see the multiplicity of systems and the disparity that sometimes exists in the installation of the same system in two different places of worship" (ANTUNES PIRES, 2007:142).
41 "... the problematic related to projection devices is not limited to the simple interactions between the device, its installation, the work and the projection site, we find in fact that certain systems are sometimes unsuitable for certain works" (ANTUNES PIRES, 2007:142).
42 "Duchenne considered that ecouter en utilisant des casques '(...) represents une variante tres interessante de l'ecoute domestique (...) par l'individualisation de l espace qu'elle cree (...)'" (ANTUNES PIRES, 2007:152).

*Figure 13: Visualization of the emitting devices: the listening points. Ilha dos Marinheiros, April 22, 2017.*

I found the speakers to be underpowered when used in a large, open space. However, their power and emission quality were sufficient for the fusion between the sounds of the landscape and the electronic sounds intended in the planning. The necessary power supply was sourced from a resident close to the installation environment. To connect the loudspeakers, the different powers and impedances of each device were taken into account in order to connect them to the 6 ohm amplifier. By connecting them in series and in parallel, the impedance achieved at each point was 6 ohms, making the most of each listening point.

As for the characteristics of the installation of the devices, the following were identified: 1. the visualization of the wires; 2. the lack of support for positioning the speakers; 3. the resistance of the wires; and 4. the unevenness of the terrain. First of all, I realized that the sight of the 75 meters of wires used to connect the devices created the expectation of a sound experience on site. However, this was not the case when approaching the fusion of recorded elements with the sounds of the landscape at the time of the performance, as it generates the expectation of overlapping materials, rather than their fusion. Furthermore, the type of connection made between the speakers promotes the formation of a fence by keeping the wires exposed. These issues could be solved by burying the wires, partially concealing them from the landscape.

Secondly, the lack of supports for positioning the speakers provides a better fit with the display environment. The absence of supports also provides possibilities for hiding the speakers and integrating the device more closely with elements of the landscape. To solve the problem of mobility, the speakers were partially buried in the sand or nailed to tree stumps. Figure 6 shows a panoramic view of the performance and positioning of the devices:

*Figure 14: Presentation Space: panoramic view of the sound installation. Ilha dos Marinheiros, April 22, 2017.*

## 9 BIBLIOGRAPHICAL REFERENCES

ANTUNES PIRES, I. 2007. *"La notion d'Espace dans la creation musicale: idees. concepts et attributions".* Universite Paris 8 - Vincennes - Saint-Denis. Doctoral thesis.

AUSTIN, L. 2000. *"Sound Diffusion in Composition and Performance: An Interview with Denis Smalley".* Computer Music Journal, 22:2, pp. 10-21, Summer 2000. Massachusetts Institute of Technology.

BANDT, R. 2006. *"Sound Installation: Blurring the Boundaries of the Eye, the Ear, Space and Time".* Contemporary Music Review, vol. 25. No. 4, August 2006, pp. 353-365. 2006

Taylor and Francis Group Ltd.

BARLOW, M. 1995. *"The Architecture of Image and Sound: Dwelling in the Work of Mary Lucier".* Summer 1995. Art Journal.

CAMPESATO, L. and IAZZETTA, F. 2006. *"Sound, space and time in sound art".* ANPPOM 2006.

CHION, M. 2012. *"The Three Listening Modes".* The Sound Studies Reader, Edited by Jonathan Sterne. Routledge, New York.

DEERY, A. 2015. *"Practical approaches towards interactivity in soundscape composition".* Queen's University Belfast.

DERRIDA, J. 1967. *"La voix etle phenomene".* Paris: Presses Universite de France.

DUHAUTPAS and SOLOMOS. 2014. *"Hildegard Westerkamp and the Ecology of Sound as Experience. Notes on Beneath the Forest Floor."* The Journal of Acoustic Ecology, Volume 13, n. 1. winter / spring 2013-2014.

DUMYAHN, S. L. and PIJANOWSKI, B. C. 2011. *"Soundscape Conservation".* Landscape Ecology, vol. 26, pp. 1327-1344, 2011.

ECO, U. 1984. *"Semiotics and Philosophy of Language".* Theory of Arts and Literature. Piaget Institute.

FASTL, H. and ZWICKER, E. 1999. "Psychoacoustics: Facts and Models. Third Edition. Springer, 2006.

FEISST, S. 2014. *"Animal Ecologies: Laurie Spiegel's musical explorations of urban wildlife".* Social Alternatives, vol. 33. no. 1, 2014.

FONTANA, B. 1987. *"The Relocation of Ambient Sound: Urban Sound Sculpture".* Leonardo, Vol. 41, No.2, pp. 154-158, 2008.

GADAMER, H. 2010. *"The Hermeneutics of the Work of Art".* Selected and translated by Marco Antonio Casanova. Editora WMF Martins Fontes Ltda.

INGOLD, T. 2000. *"The Perception of the Environment - Essays in livinghood, dwelling and skilf'.* London: Routledge, 2000.

KELLER, D. 2000. *"Compositional Processes from an Ecological Perspective".* Ways and Means, Leonardo Music Journal, vol.10, pp. 55-60, 2000.

LaBELLE, B. 2006. *"Background Noise: Perspectives on Sound Art.* The Continuum Publishing Group Ltd. New York.

LEPPERT, R. 2012. *"Reading the sonoric landscape".* The Sound Studies Reader, Edited by Jonathan Sterne. Routledge, New York.

MACEDO, F. 2011. "PHENOMENOLOGY, SPATIAL MUSIC AND THE COMPOSER: PRELUDE TO A PHENOMENOLOGY OF SPACE IN ELECTROACOUSTIC MUSIC". *Proceedings of the International Computer Music Conference 2011, University of Huddersfield, UK, July 31 - August 5.*

McCARTNEY, A. 1999. *"Sounding Places: Situated Conversations through the Soundscape composition of Hildegard Westerkamp".* PhD;
Toronto.

MOHR, H. 2007. *"Listening and moving in the urban environment",* Women & Performance: ajournal offeministtheory, 17:2, 185-203.

POLLI, A. 2011. *"Soundscape, Bonification, and sound activism".* AI & Society, vol.27, pp. 257-268. 2012.

REYBROUCK, M. 2004. *"Music Cognition, Semiotics and the Experience of Time: Ontosemantical and Epistemological Claims".* Journal of New Music Research, Vol. 33, No. 4. pp. 411-428. 2004 Taylor and Francis Group Ltd.

RICOEUR, P. 2008. *"Hermeneutics and Ideologies".* Organization, translation and presentation: Hilton Japiassu. Editora Vozes, Petropolis 2008.

SANTAELLA, L. and NOTH, W. 1997. *"IMAGE: Cognition, Semiotics, Media".* Editora Iluminuras Ltda. 2014.

SCHAFER, R. M. 1977. *"The Tuning of the World".* Translated by Marisa Trench Fonterrada. Editora Unesp.

SMALLEY, D. 1997. *"Spectromorphology: explaining sound-shapes".* Organized Sound 2(2): 107-26. 1997 Cambridge University Press. United Kingdom.

SMALLEY, D. 2007. *"Space-form and the acousmatic image".* Organized Sound, 12 (1). CUP, 2007.

TRUAX, B. 1996. *"Soundscape, Acoustic Communication and Environmental Sound Composition".* Contemporary Music Review, vol. 15, 1-2, pp. 49-65.

VAGGIONE, H. 1998. *"L'espace composable. Sur quelques categories operatoires dans la musique electroacoustique".* L'Espace : Musique / Philosophie. Textes reunis et presentes par Jean - Marc CHOUVEL et Makis SOLOMOS. Paris: L'Harmattan, 1998. Collection Musique et Philosophie. pp. 154- 166.

VOORVELT, M. 1997. *"The envoronmental element in Barry Truax compositions".* Journal of New Music Research. Routledge.

WESTERKAMP, H. 1988. *"Listening and Soundmaking:A study ofmusic-as-environment".* Master's Thesis; Simon Fraser University.

WESTERKAMP, H. 1974. "Soundwalking", Sound Heritage, Vol. III No. 4 (1974). Reprinted and updated in Angus Carlyle (ed.), *Autumn Leaves: Sound and the Environment in Artistic Practice* (Paris, 2007), pp. 49-54.

WISHART, T. 1996. *"On sonic art".* Amsterdam: Harwood Academic Publishers, 1996.

MIX
Papier aus verantwortungsvollen Quellen
Paper from responsible sources
FSC® C105338

Printed by Books on Demand GmbH, Norderstedt / Germany